The "Digital India" Paradox

INDIA MATTERS, Volume 1

G.K.MENON

Published by G.K.MENON, 2025.

THE "DIGITAL INDIA" PARADOX

First edition. December 31, 2025.

ISBN: 979-8233505157

Written by G.K.MENON.

Also by G.K.MENON

INDIA MATTERS
The "Digital India" Paradox
Savarkar The Non-Defeatable
False Prophets of Ambedkarism

The Cognition Series
The Starforge Protocol
The Neural Covenent
Beyond Neural Axis
The Omega Protocol

The Research & Analysis Series
The Manufactured Mind
The Jews The Most Haunted People on Earth

The "Digital India" Paradox

The "Digital India" Paradox

By

G.K.Menon

This book is written under the pen name G. K. Menon.
First published in 2025

Foreword: The Pulse of a New Reality

For centuries, the story of India was written in ink, on paper, and across the dust of its vast landscapes. It was a story of slow, deliberate movements—of postcards that took weeks to arrive and queues that stretched into seasons. But in the span of a single decade, that story has been rewritten in binary.

Today, India is the site of the most ambitious digital experiment in human history. We are a nation that has bypassed the gradual evolution of the West, leaping from a cash-heavy, document-reliant society straight into a world of biometric identities, instant cloud payments, and AI-governed labor. This is the "Software Miracle." It has brought the marginalized into the light of the formal economy and turned the humble smartphone into a tool of unprecedented power.

But every miracle has its friction.

As an investigative journey, The Silicon Pulse does not look at India through the rose-tinted lens of a corporate brochure, nor through the cynical eyes of a critic. Instead, it looks through the lens of the paradox. We explore an India where a street vendor accepts digital payments while standing in a "shadow zone" of connectivity; where a young engineer builds the global future of AI while fearing his own obsolescence; and where the ease of a one-click life coexists with the sophisticated shadows of the "Jamtara Frequency."

The "Silicon Pulse" is the heartbeat of a nation in transition. It is fast, it is chaotic, and it is undeniably vibrant. But a pulse that beats too fast can lead to burnout, and a pulse that is ignored can lead to a silent crisis.

This book is an investigation into that heartbeat. It is a guide to understanding how 1.4 billion people are navigating the "glitches" in the system to build something entirely new. We delve into the human cost of the gig economy, the high-stakes battle for data sovereignty, and the invisible architecture of surveillance. More importantly, we search for the "Tomorrow Protocol"—the roadmap to a digital society that values safety as much as speed, and human dignity as much as high-speed data.

Whether you are a technologist, a policymaker, or a citizen holding a smartphone, this book is about the world you are currently building. It is an invitation to look beneath the screen, to unmask the friction, and to ensure that as India pulses into the future, it does so without losing its soul.

Chapter 1-The Zero-Rupee Leap

1.1 A Shop Where Time Lingers but Money Does Not

The humidity in Old Delhi's Khari Baoli market has a way of slowing time. It thickens the air, presses against the skin, and gives the impression that centuries coexist in the same narrow alley. Burlap sacks of spices—chilies, turmeric, cumin, coriander—line the walls like relics of a mercantile civilization that long predates the modern state. Their scent is heavy, stinging, and persistent, clinging to memory as much as to clothing.

Ramesh's shop occupies barely more space than a walk-in closet. A wooden counter, polished smooth by three generations of hands, divides seller from buyer. Above it hangs a portrait of his grandfather, who conducted business in a world governed by cash, reputation, and handwritten *parchas*—paper slips that served as both ledger and promise. Money was physical then, counted by touch and sight, its movement slow and deliberate.

Below that portrait, taped to a concrete pillar with frayed Scotch tape, is a small laminated plastic square: a QR code.

A customer in a sweat-stained shirt leans forward, scans it with a cracked smartphone, types in "450," and waits. Three seconds later, a robotic female voice chirps from a small blue speaker resting on a sack of cumin:

"Received four hundred and fifty rupees on PhonePe."

This is the sound of the Zero-Rupee Leap.

In less time than it once took to count four currency notes, Ramesh's shop traverses centuries. No cash drawer opens. No credit card terminal hums. No receipt prints. There is no transaction fee deducted from the merchant, no plastic intermediary, no delayed settlement. The exchange is instant, invisible, and final.

This moment captures what many describe as India's software miracle—the decision not to replicate Western financial systems, but to bypass them entirely. Yet within this apparent triumph lies a question that does not surface at the counter: the payment felt free, but was it truly without cost?

1.2 The Architecture of the Stack: When Money Became Language

To understand the Zero-Rupee Leap, one must look beneath the QR code to the infrastructure that enables it. For decades, global finance operated through proprietary rails. Payment systems were walled gardens. If one held a particular card, one traveled through that company's network. Banks owned both the rails and the customer relationship, and interoperability was limited, expensive, and carefully controlled.

In 2016, India introduced the Unified Payments Interface. UPI was not an application, nor a corporation. It was a protocol—a shared language that allowed banks, payment apps, and users to communicate seamlessly. A cooperative bank in rural Bihar could transact instantly with a technology platform headquartered in Bengaluru.

This was not merely a technical upgrade. It was a reconfiguration of power. By turning money into data—structured, routable, and nearly weightless—the system stripped traditional banks of their gatekeeping role and elevated software as the primary interface between citizen and state-regulated finance.

The political significance of this shift is often understated. When transactions become instantaneous and nearly costless, the locus of control moves away from institutions that manage delay and toward systems that manage data. Efficiency improves dramatically, but visibility expands at the same rate. Every transaction becomes legible, traceable, and archivable by default.

The Stack did not simply modernize payments. It redefined what money is in practice: no longer a physical bearer instrument, but a data packet moving across interoperable systems. This transformation laid the foundation for unprecedented inclusion—and for unprecedented observation.

1.3 The End of Cash: Inclusion Through Friction Removal

In India, cash was never merely a medium of exchange. It was autonomy. It functioned without electricity, internet access, or literacy. It allowed participation in economic life without exposure to administrative oversight. For millions, cash represented not evasion, but resilience.

When digital payments were introduced at scale, skepticism was immediate and justified. How could a country with frequent power cuts, uneven connectivity, and vast digital illiteracy trust invisible money? The answer did not arrive through persuasion or ideology. It arrived through friction removal.

The revolution did not begin in shopping malls or corporate offices. It began at tea stalls, vegetable carts, and auto-rickshaw stands. The constant struggle for small change—the absence of five-rupee coins, the disputes over exact amounts—vanished with a QR code. By eliminating merchant transaction fees, the system inverted traditional incentives. Going digital became cheaper than staying analog.

Slowly, the informal economy began to emit a digital pulse. Ten-rupee teas, twenty-rupee rides, and five-hundred-rupee grain purchases started leaving data trails. What had once existed beyond formal accounting entered a system of continuous recording.

This was inclusion, but it was inclusion on the system's terms. Participation no longer required trust in the state, but it did require submission to its digital infrastructure.

1.4 The Unwritten Contract Behind the Zero-Rupee Promise

To Ramesh, the blue speaker represents reliability. It announces certainty. He does not think in terms of protocols, databases, or policy frameworks. He sees only that the system works.

Yet the Zero-Rupee Leap came with an unwritten contract. The friction did not disappear; it was displaced. It moved away from the point of transaction and embedded itself elsewhere—in data retention, profiling, and aggregation.

Every payment carries more than value. It carries time, location, frequency, and behavioral signals. Over months and years, these signals accumulate into detailed economic portraits. Cash once dissolved into anonymity once exchanged. Digital money persists.

As the silicon pulse spread across the subcontinent, new questions emerged quietly, almost invisibly. Who else listens when the blue speaker speaks? Where is the transaction stored, and for how long? Who can access it, correlate it, or act upon it? Through which systems does that 450 rupees travel before settling into Ramesh's account?

The leap was real. The efficiency undeniable.

But the cost was deferred.

And deferred costs, in political systems as in financial ones, rarely disappear. They return—later, quietly, and with consequences.

Chapter 2-The ID Mandate: Inclusion or Intrusiveness?

If UPI is the blood of India's digital body, then Aadhaar is its skeleton. It gives the system structure, reach, and rigidity. Without it, digital governance would collapse into disconnected platforms. With it, the state gains a single, unified framework through which identity can be verified, benefits distributed, and citizens rendered legible to authority. Yet skeletons do not bend easily. What provides form can also constrain movement.

2.1 The 12-Digit Anchor: Mapping a Billion Souls

Before the turn toward biometric identity, millions of Indians lived in a condition best described as documentary invisibility. They existed socially, economically, and politically, yet lacked the formal proofs that modern states demand. No birth certificates, no permanent addresses, no standardized names spelled consistently across documents. For the migrant worker, the elderly widow, the landless laborer, identity was relational rather than bureaucratic—known to neighbors, employers, and local officials, but rarely to the state itself.

This invisibility carried real consequences. Without documents, individuals could not open bank accounts, obtain SIM cards, or reliably access welfare benefits to which they were legally entitled. Public Distribution System rations leaked through layers of intermediaries. "Ghost beneficiaries" proliferated—names on paper unmoored from living bodies—draining the treasury and eroding trust in state capacity. The problem was not merely corruption, but fragmentation. Identity was scattered across thousands of local registers, none of which spoke to each other.

Aadhaar was conceived as a solution to this fragmentation. Introduced in 2009, it promised a single, portable identity—one number, one person—anchored in the body itself. Biometrics bypassed the unreliability of names and addresses. Ten fingerprints and two iris scans would do what paper never could: establish uniqueness at scale. A migrant from Bihar could authenticate himself in Bengaluru as easily as in his home village. Geography would no longer determine recognition.

In conception, Aadhaar was elegant. It replaced trust in intermediaries with trust in infrastructure. By centralizing identity verification, the state could deposit benefits directly into bank accounts, cutting out layers of rent-seeking bureaucracy. Welfare could become precise rather than approximate. Inclusion would no longer depend on local discretion.

The scale of the project was unprecedented. No other country had attempted biometric identification across such a vast, diverse population. In policy circles, Aadhaar was hailed as a masterstroke—a digital anchor that could stabilize governance in a society long undermined by informality. Identity became foundational infrastructure, upon which payments, telecommunications, healthcare, and subsidies could be layered.

Yet the very ambition that made Aadhaar powerful also made it unforgiving. A single anchor point creates coherence, but it also creates dependency. When identity is centralized, failure is no longer local and recoverable; it becomes systemic. The promise of inclusion was absolute—but so was the cost of exclusion.

2.2 The Ghost in the Database: When the Algorithm Says "No"

The scene shifts from policy documents and data centers to a dusty government outpost in rural Jharkhand. A queue of villagers stretches under the sparse shade of a neem tree. At the front stands Lakshmi, seventy years old, her body bearing the marks of decades of manual labor. She is not here to vote. She is not here to apply for a loan. She is here to prove she exists.

Lakshmi presses her thumb against a biometric scanner. The glass glows blue, then red. "Authentication Failed."

For the system, this is a technical event. For Lakshmi, it is existential. In a digital-first welfare architecture, authentication is not a formality; it is a gate. When the gate does not open, benefits do not flow. Grain is withheld. Pensions stall. The state does not punish actively; it simply withholds recognition.

Biometric failure is not an anomaly. Manual labor wears down fingerprints. Age alters skin elasticity. Cataracts cloud iris scans. The very populations Aadhaar was designed to empower—the elderly, agricultural workers, construction laborers—are statistically the most likely to fail biometric authentication. What was meant to eliminate discretion has introduced a new, colder arbiter: the algorithm.

Unlike a local official, the algorithm cannot be persuaded. It does not recognize hunger, fatigue, or history. It recognizes only match or mismatch. When it fails, there is often no immediate human authority empowered to override it. Appeals are slow, opaque, and procedurally dense. In the meantime, life continues—but benefits do not.

These are the "biometric ghosts": individuals who exist physically but are denied digitally. They are not undocumented; they are over-documented, reduced to a single failing parameter. The tragedy lies in the inversion. Identity, once flexible and negotiated, has become rigid and absolute. There is no partial recognition, no provisional acceptance.

Investigations into welfare-linked Aadhaar failures have documented cases where authentication errors translated directly into starvation and destitution. The system does not intend harm, but intention is irrelevant when architecture produces predictable exclusion. A technical safeguard becomes a moral hazard when it is deployed without redundancy.

The digital state prides itself on precision. But precision without mercy is not justice; it is automation of denial.

2.3 The Privacy Question: Who Owns the Body as Data?

Beyond village outposts and ration shops, Aadhaar triggered a different confrontation—one that unfolded in courtrooms and constitutional benches. When the state collects fingerprints and iris scans, it is not merely identifying citizens; it is storing biological markers that cannot be changed, revoked, or replaced. A password can be reset. A fingerprint cannot.

This realization ignited one of the most consequential debates in modern Indian jurisprudence, culminating in landmark judgments by the Supreme Court of India on the Right to Privacy. The core question was not technological, but philosophical: What is the boundary between governance and intrusion in a digital society?

Proponents argued that data was secure, purpose-limited, and essential for inclusion. Critics countered that linking Aadhaar across banking, telecommunications, taxation, and welfare created a system of total traceability. When identity becomes universal and mandatory, anonymity ceases to exist in practice—even if it exists in law.

The danger is not a single act of surveillance, but aggregation. Each database may be benign in isolation. Together, they form a comprehensive behavioral map. Spending patterns, location histories, social connections—all become correlatable. The "Silicon Pulse" never truly fades.

Privacy in this context is not secrecy; it is autonomy. It is the ability to exist without constant legibility to power. Aadhaar shifted the default from opacity to transparency, without fully resolving who controls that transparency and for what ends.

As Lakshmi's fingerprint finally matches and the scanner flashes green, the system records success. She receives her rice. The miracle works. Yet in that moment, something else is deposited—another permanent data point in a system that remembers long after hunger is forgotten.

The question this chapter leaves unresolved is not whether Aadhaar works. It does. The question is whether a society should build governance on an identity system that cannot forget, forgive, or fail gracefully.

In the chapters that follow, we will examine how this skeletal structure—rigid, efficient, and unforgiving—reshaped the relationship between the Indian citizen and the digital state.

Chapter 3-The Jamtara Frequency: The New Frontier of Fraud

While the glass towers of Bengaluru celebrated the triumph of India's software revolution, a parallel innovation was unfolding far from air-conditioned campuses and venture capital boardrooms. In the eucalyptus-lined interiors of Jharkhand, particularly in the district of Jamtara, the Silicon Pulse acquired a darker rhythm. Here, the digital leap did not translate into prosperity or inclusion. It translated into opportunity of a different kind.

This chapter examines how India's accelerated digitization created a structural "trust gap"—a space between technological capability and social preparedness—into which an entire underground economy has inserted itself.

3.1 Social Engineering: The Art of the Digital Heist

The contemporary digital heist does not begin with a breach of firewalls or the cracking of encrypted databases. It begins with a phone call. Somewhere in Punjab, a farmer pauses his work. In Chennai, a retired schoolteacher answers an unfamiliar number. The voice on the other end is calm, authoritative, and urgent.

"Sir, your KYC is expiring. Your account will be blocked in ten minutes. Please download this application to verify."

This is not hacking in the conventional sense. It is social engineering—the deliberate manipulation of human psychology to bypass technical security. The scammer does not attack the server; he attacks trust. Encryption remains intact. Protocols function perfectly. It is the human user who is induced to open the gate.

In Jamtara, this craft has been refined into an industry. Investigations reveal clusters of young men operating from modest mud-brick houses, seated on plastic chairs, smartphones in hand, headsets plugged in. Their workdays resemble those of call-center employees. Leads are managed.

Scripts are memorized. Success rates are tracked. Payments are performance-based.

The language they deploy is drawn directly from the vocabulary of the digital state. Words like "UPI," "KYC," "verification," and "security update" are weaponized. The scammer mirrors the tone of legitimate authority, exploiting the citizen's conditioning to comply with official-sounding instructions. The very success of digital governance—its emphasis on urgency, alerts, and compliance—becomes the scammer's most effective tool.

The sophistication lies not in technology but in timing. Scammers track news cycles, banking updates, and policy announcements. When regulations change, phishing scripts change with them. The attack surface is not a vulnerability in code; it is the cognitive overload of a population adjusting to constant digital demands.

In this ecosystem, UPI and related tools are not compromised; they are repurposed. Screen-sharing applications—designed for remote assistance—become instruments of theft. Once access is granted, the transaction is initiated by the victim's own hand. From the system's perspective, nothing illegal has occurred. Authentication was valid. Consent was given.

This is the central irony of the Jamtara phenomenon. The crime operates entirely within the rules of the system. The fraud is social, not technical. And because it exploits trust rather than breaches security, it is extraordinarily difficult to prevent through code alone.

3.2 The Literacy Gap: Connectivity Without Defensive Capacity

At the heart of the Jamtara frequency lies a structural imbalance: the Digital Literacy Gap. India connected hundreds of millions of citizens to the internet in under a decade. Smartphones became ubiquitous. Data became cheap. Financial services became app-based. But digital skepticism—the instinct to doubt, verify, and resist—did not scale at the same speed.

For first-generation internet users, visual cues substitute for judgment. A professional interface implies legitimacy. A blue tick signals authority. An automated voice response conveys authenticity. The phone is perceived as a device for entertainment and communication, not as a gateway to one's financial identity.

This gap creates a lopsided battlefield. On one side are scam networks that operate full-time, studying banking workflows, platform updates, and user behavior with obsessive focus. On the other side is a population encountering digital finance episodically, often under stress, often without guidance.

The Zero-Rupee Leap removed transactional friction, but it also removed protective pauses. Cash transactions required physical presence and time. Digital transactions demand speed and decisiveness. The cognitive load is high, particularly for elderly users and those unfamiliar with financial interfaces.

Educational campaigns exist, but they are abstract and episodic. Warnings arrive after losses, not before. Instructions are generic, while scams are personalized. The asymmetry is structural. The scammer's livelihood depends on mastery. The citizen's vulnerability is incidental.

This is not merely a failure of awareness; it is a failure of sequencing. Technology arrived before culture adapted. Connectivity preceded caution. The result is a digitally exposed population—connected, included, and profoundly vulnerable.

3.3 Hard-Coding Trust: Can the Stack Defend Against the Human Factor?

As losses mounted, attention shifted back to the architects of the system. Could trust be hard-coded? Could software compensate for human fallibility?

The investigation moves into cybercrime units, where detectives attempt to trace money that moves faster than paperwork ever could. In cramped offices in Gurugram and other urban centers, officers track transaction chains that traverse dozens of accounts in seconds. Money is fragmented, laundered through "mule accounts," and reassembled elsewhere before alerts are even triggered.

The speed that made UPI revolutionary also makes fraud recovery nearly impossible. The system is optimized for finality. Once transferred, funds settle instantly. Reversibility—essential for justice—is sacrificed for efficiency.

Design interventions are debated: transaction delays, spending caps, behavioral alerts. But each safeguard introduces friction, and friction undermines the very promise of the digital leap. The architects face an inescapable dilemma: a system optimized for trust is inherently vulnerable to its exploitation.

The deeper issue is philosophical. Digital India assumed that trust could be embedded in infrastructure. Jamtara demonstrates that trust remains a social phenomenon. Code can authenticate identity, but it cannot authenticate intent.

The chapter closes with an unresolved tension. In a society where screens mediate authority, how does one teach citizens to distrust convincingly rendered falsehoods? How does a state protect users without infantilizing them or slowing the system into irrelevance?

The Jamtara Frequency is not an anomaly. It is a signal. It reminds us that the most dangerous friction in a digital society is not latency or downtime—it is misplaced trust. And until that gap is addressed, the miracle will continue to cast long shadows.

Chapter 4-Algorithmic Feudalism: The Gig Economy Shift

If one stands on a street corner in **Bengaluru**, **Mumbai**, or **Gurugram** for more than a minute, the pattern reveals itself. A flash of electric orange cuts through traffic. Neon green waits at a signal. Primary red idles beside a curb. These are not random colors; they are uniforms. Together, they form the most visible workforce of Digital India—the Gig Army.

They are the delivery partners, ride-hailers, and logistics workers who translate software promises into physical motion. Their labor is the final mile of the digital miracle. Without them, platforms are merely code and capital. With them, apps become habits, expectations, and dependencies.

This chapter examines the invisible architecture governing this workforce. It argues that beneath the language of flexibility and entrepreneurship lies a new labor regime—Algorithmic Feudalism—where control is exerted not through foremen or contracts, but through ratings, timers, and opaque formulas.

4.1 The Ten-Minute Race: Speed as Structural Violence

The promise of the platform economy is convenience. Groceries in ten minutes. A cab in three. Food before hunger has fully formed. To the consumer, this speed feels frictionless—almost magical. To the worker, speed is not a benefit; it is an obligation enforced by countdowns.

Sunil is twenty-four. He migrated from a village in Maharashtra to Pune with a borrowed motorcycle and a smartphone. On his handlebars is a phone mount. On the screen is a timer. His working day is not structured by hours but by seconds. Every assignment begins with a countdown, every delay is logged, and every deviation is penalized.

The investigation leads into the "dark stores" that make instant delivery possible—windowless micro-warehouses hidden in basements and repurposed residential spaces. Inside, workers pack items under relentless pressure, guided by handheld scanners and automated prompts. There are no customers here, only clocks. The design is deliberate. By shrinking physical distance and compressing time, platforms externalize risk onto workers.

As delivery windows shrink, the margin for human variability disappears. Traffic congestion, weather, mechanical failure, fatigue—none of these are accommodated by the algorithm. Speed becomes non-negotiable. The miracle of instant gratification is built on elevated accident risk, physical exhaustion, and constant vigilance.

This is not accidental; it is structural. The platform's competitive advantage depends on speed. Speed depends on risk. And risk is borne almost entirely by workers classified as "partners," not employees. The absence of formal employment status allows platforms to avoid liability for injuries, insurance, or downtime.

The ten-minute race reveals a deeper truth about digital efficiency: when time is optimized for consumers, it is weaponized against labor. What is marketed as convenience is experienced as compression. The clock does not merely measure work; it disciplines it.

4.2 Managed by Code: Life Under Algorithmic Authority

In traditional employment, control is personal. A supervisor can be argued with, negotiated against, or appealed to. In the gig economy, control is abstract. Sunil does not have a manager; he has an interface. His performance is evaluated not by judgment, but by metrics.

This is management by algorithm. Routes are assigned by GPS optimization. Pay fluctuates based on dynamic pricing formulas. Access to future work depends on ratings averaged to a single decimal point. A score below 4.5 can mean fewer orders. Below 4.2 can mean deactivation.

The psychological toll of this system is profound. The worker is constantly visible but never heard. GPS tracking converts movement into data. Pauses become "idle time." Deviations become inefficiency. Helping an accident victim or stopping for repairs registers not as virtue, but as delay.

This is friction at its most intimate level. The algorithm does not understand context. It understands compliance. Empathy is not a parameter. When a worker falls ill or faces an emergency, the system registers absence, not reason.

Platforms employ sophisticated behavioral design to sustain this compliance. Gamification—badges, streaks, surge incentives—nudges workers to stay logged in longer, accept riskier hours, and work during adverse conditions. Rainstorms and late nights are reframed as "earning opportunities."

The language is motivational; the reality is coercive. Because income is unpredictable and piece-rated, workers feel compelled to chase incentives even when exhausted. Declining orders can reduce visibility. Logging off too often can lower "reliability scores."

This form of control is more effective than traditional supervision because it is internalized. The worker monitors himself. Anxiety replaces oversight. Discipline becomes self-imposed.

Algorithmic management thus represents a shift in power. Authority is no longer exercised through command, but through calculation. The worker cannot negotiate with math. He can only comply—or disappear.

4.3 The Future of Labor: Dignity, Rights, and Resistance

As the gig economy expands, a global debate intensifies: are gig workers entrepreneurs or employees? Platforms insist on the former, emphasizing flexibility and choice. Reality suggests something closer to dependence without protection.

India has become the world's largest laboratory for this experiment. Millions rely on gig work as primary income. Yet labor protections remain tied to twentieth-century definitions of employment. Health insurance, paid leave, accident compensation, and collective bargaining often do not apply.

In response, workers are adapting. A new phenomenon has emerged—the unionization of the cloud. Delivery riders and drivers organize through WhatsApp groups, Telegram channels, and social media. Information about pay changes spreads rapidly. Log-off strikes are coordinated digitally. Ratings are discussed collectively.

This resistance highlights the central contradiction of Algorithmic Feudalism. Platforms rely on decentralized labor, yet workers share common grievances. The same networks that deliver food now deliver dissent.

Legal systems struggle to keep pace. Courts debate whether algorithmic control constitutes employment. Policymakers face pressure to preserve innovation while preventing exploitation. Platforms warn that regulation will slow growth. Workers counter that growth without dignity is extraction.

The chapter concludes with a sobering recognition. Digital India has not merely created new jobs; it has reorganized labor relations. The app has replaced the landlord, the factory, and the foreman. But unlike traditional feudalism, this system offers no stable obligation—only conditional access.

The Silicon Pulse beats powerfully, but unevenly. It rewards those who place orders and penalizes those who fulfill them. Whether this pulse can be recalibrated to include dignity, security, and voice remains one of the defining questions of India's digital future.

Chapter 5-The Deepfake Republic: Truth in the Age of AI

In early 2024, a video began circulating across social media platforms in India. A long-deceased political patriarch appeared seated in his familiar attire, posture unmistakable, voice calm and authoritative. He looked directly into the camera and endorsed a candidate in the upcoming elections. For millions of viewers, the effect was uncanny—less deception than resurrection. To those trained in digital media, it was something else entirely: a deepfake.

This chapter examines how India has become the world's most volatile laboratory for synthetic media. While the tools of generative artificial intelligence were largely developed elsewhere, India supplied something far more decisive: scale, velocity, and belief. Here, the Silicon Pulse does not merely move money, labor, or identity—it reshapes perception itself. In a society where visual proof has long been synonymous with truth, the collapse of visual evidence introduces a crisis deeper than misinformation. It introduces epistemic instability.

5.1 The Death of Evidence: Life in a Post-Verification Internet

The investigation begins far from the screens where deepfakes are consumed, in the back offices of political consultancies, digital marketing firms, and informal "IT cells" scattered across the outskirts of Delhi and Hyderabad. These spaces do not resemble criminal dens. They resemble start-ups. Young operators sit before laptops, toggling between generative video tools, voice-cloning software, and prompt libraries refined through trial and error.

What has changed fundamentally is the cost of deception. A decade ago, fabricating a convincing video required sophisticated equipment, skilled technicians, and substantial capital. Today, a subscription-priced AI model and a mid-range laptop are sufficient. Generative systems can reconstruct a person's face, voice, and mannerisms from minutes of publicly available footage. The barrier to entry has collapsed.

This technological shift has produced what can only be described as the death of evidence. Video—once the strongest form of proof—has become suspect by default. Audio recordings can be forged. Images can be synthesized. Even live video calls are no longer immune to manipulation.

The implications are legal as much as cultural. India's evidentiary frameworks evolved in a world where physical artifacts and recorded media were difficult to falsify at scale. Courts, investigators, and journalists relied on audiovisual material as corroboration. Synthetic media erodes that foundation. When every piece of evidence can be dismissed as fabricated, truth becomes negotiable.

The problem deepens when consent is considered. The "Consent Gap" is one of the most underexamined consequences of generative AI. Faces and voices are scraped from social media, film clips, interviews, and private accounts. They are recombined into pornographic material, fraudulent endorsements, or fabricated crimes—often without the victim ever knowing until damage is done. Bollywood actresses and college students occupy the same vulnerability space: visibility without control.

Law struggles to keep pace because the crime does not occur in a physical location. It occurs in what developers call "latent space"—a probabilistic realm where outputs are generated statistically rather than authored directly. Responsibility becomes diffuse. Was the crime committed by the user, the model, the platform, or the data source? Existing statutes offer no clear answers.

What emerges is a society where verification is no longer assumed. The burden shifts from proving falsity to proving authenticity—and that burden is far heavier.

5.2 WhatsApp Universities: Velocity, Fear, and the Collapse of Skepticism

If artificial intelligence is the engine of synthetic media, WhatsApp is its transmission system. With over 500 million users in India, WhatsApp is not merely a messaging application; it is the country's most powerful information infrastructure. News, rumor, warning, and propaganda flow through it without editorial filtration.

The investigative focus here is not technology but psychology. India's digital expansion created millions of "digital migrants"—citizens who moved from minimal connectivity to full smartphone immersion in a matter of months. For many, the phone is not a supplement to other media; it is the primary interface with the world.

In this environment, confirmation bias becomes a force multiplier. Messages that align with preexisting fears, identities, or loyalties are not questioned; they are forwarded. A deepfake video warning of child-lifters, communal violence, or imminent government action is received not as content to be evaluated, but as an emergency to be acted upon.

The velocity of WhatsApp ensures that reaction precedes reflection. Fact-checking operates on hours or days. Viral fear operates on minutes. By the time authorities or journalists respond, real-world consequences—panic, violence, reputational destruction—may already have occurred.

Unlike open platforms, WhatsApp's encryption prevents external monitoring. This design protects privacy but also shields misinformation. Falsehoods do not need to persuade everyone; they need only to circulate within closed, trusted networks.

This is the paradox of digital intimacy. Messages received from friends or family carry implicit credibility. When synthetic media enters these channels, skepticism collapses. The lie is no longer external; it arrives embedded in trust.

The result is a media ecosystem where belief is detached from verification. Truth becomes secondary to emotional plausibility. The Silicon Pulse accelerates perception without strengthening discernment.

5.3 The AI Arms Race: Fact-Checking in an Asymmetric War

The final section of this chapter moves to the cyber-frontline: independent fact-checking organizations such as Alt News and Boom Live. In modest offices, small teams analyze viral content frame by frame, searching for anomalies—a distorted shadow, an unnatural blink, a mismatched lip movement.

These investigators function as digital surgeons, operating under relentless time pressure. Their work is meticulous, technical, and emotionally exhausting. For every manipulated video they debunk, dozens more circulate unchecked.

The asymmetry is structural. Generative models improve continuously. Every exposed flaw becomes training data for the next iteration. Fact-checkers operate reactively; AI systems operate evolutionarily. The cost of creation decreases while the cost of verification increases.

This imbalance has prompted calls for systemic interventions: cryptographic watermarking of AI-generated content, mandatory disclosure of synthetic media, and platform liability for algorithmic amplification. Yet implementation lags behind innovation. Platforms resist accountability, citing scale and technical complexity. Governments debate regulation while elections proceed under conditions of informational uncertainty.

The deeper crisis is philosophical. Democratic systems presume a shared factual baseline. When citizens cannot agree on what they are seeing, deliberation collapses. Skepticism turns corrosive. Every exposure of a fake paradoxically strengthens the claim that "nothing can be trusted."

As this chapter closes, the Deepfake Republic reveals its most troubling implication. A society built on data, platforms, and digital trust cannot function if reality itself is programmable. The Digital Miracle depends on confidence—in systems, in institutions, and in evidence. When that confidence dissolves, efficiency becomes irrelevant.

If we can no longer trust our eyes, the question is no longer about technology. It is about the future of collective belief.

Chapter 6-Data Sovereignty: The Battle for the Indian Mind

If the twentieth century was defined by the struggle for land, resources, and oil, the twenty-first is being shaped by a quieter but more consequential contest: the struggle for data sovereignty. Territory is no longer measured only in square kilometers but in server capacity, data flows, and algorithmic influence. The borders that matter now are invisible, enforced not by armies but by infrastructure.

This chapter moves away from streets and screens and into high-security data centers, regulatory chambers, and diplomatic backchannels. It examines a central question confronting modern India: who owns the digital exhaust of 1.4 billion lives? As India generates trillions of data points each day—through payments, location tracking, communication, and consumption—data has ceased to be a byproduct of economic activity. It has become the activity itself.

6.1 Digital Colonization: When the Indian Mind Became Raw Material

For much of the last two decades, India's digital expansion unfolded under an unspoken assumption: data could flow freely across borders because the internet itself was borderless. Indian users signed up, logged in, searched, liked, shared, and paid. The data generated by these actions traveled silently to distant cloud servers, predominantly owned and operated by foreign technology companies.

This flow was rarely questioned. In the early years, the trade appeared benign. Indian consumers received free or low-cost services—search, social networking, email, navigation—in exchange for their attention and information. But over time, the scale of extraction became clear. Indian data was not merely being stored; it was being refined. It trained recommendation engines, language models, facial recognition systems, and advertising algorithms that formed the backbone of global technology empires.

This is what critics have come to describe as digital colonization. Unlike historical colonialism, it does not rely on physical occupation or coercion. It operates through convenience and consent forms few read. The raw material is behavioral data—how Indians speak, move, buy, vote, and believe. The finished products are AI systems monetized globally.

The economic imbalance is subtle but profound. India supplies the data, but the value addition occurs elsewhere. The profits accrue to companies headquartered in California, while the data subjects remain consumers rather than stakeholders. The Indian mind becomes a training dataset.

Policy-makers in New Delhi have begun to question this arrangement. If data is a strategic national asset, they argue, then exporting it freely undermines long-term sovereignty. The analogy often invoked is industrial: no nation would export crude oil indefinitely without developing domestic refining capacity. Why should data be different?

The friction here is not merely economic; it is philosophical. Data reflects culture, language, social norms, and political behavior. Allowing foreign entities to dominate its processing and interpretation risks outsourcing cognitive infrastructure. Algorithms trained on Indian behavior shape what Indians see, hear, and prioritize—often without local accountability.

The pushback against digital colonization marks a turning point. India is no longer content to be the world's largest user base. It seeks to become an owner, a processor, and a rule-setter in the data economy. But reclaiming sovereignty over data raises a new set of risks—especially when the state positions itself as the primary custodian.

6.2 The Data Fortress: Security, Localization, and the Risk of a Digital Silo

To defend this new territory, the Indian state has begun constructing what can best be described as a data fortress. The legal cornerstone of this effort is the Digital Personal Data Protection framework, alongside data localization mandates requiring certain categories of data to be stored and processed within India's borders.

The rationale is straightforward. Data stored domestically is subject to Indian law. It can be accessed for legitimate national security needs. It is less vulnerable to foreign surveillance and extraterritorial legal demands. In a world where cyber warfare and information influence have become routine, data localization is framed as defensive necessity.

This position has placed India in direct confrontation with global technology companies such as **Meta**, **Google**, and **X**. From their perspective, localization increases costs, fragments global operations, and undermines the efficiencies of cloud computing. From the state's perspective, resistance to localization signals an unwillingness to submit to sovereign regulation.

The legal and policy debates play out in sterile boardrooms and regulatory war rooms, but their implications are expansive. Data localization promises control, but it also centralizes power. When data remains within national borders, the question of access becomes unavoidable: who inside the fortress holds the keys?

Critics warn of the "splinternet"—a fractured global internet where data flows are constrained by national boundaries. Innovation thrives on scale, interoperability, and cross-border collaboration. Startups fear that excessive regulation will entrench incumbents who can afford compliance while stifling smaller players.

There is also a civil liberties dimension. Localization strengthens the state's ability to surveil and intervene. While justified in the language of security, such powers can be repurposed. The same infrastructure that keeps foreign actors out can make domestic citizens more legible than ever before.

The data fortress thus embodies a paradox. It promises sovereignty, but risks overreach. It protects national interests, but may weaken individual autonomy. The challenge is not technical but constitutional: how to balance collective security with personal privacy in an age where data is inseparable from identity.

6.3 Exporting the Stack: Soft Power and the Global South

The story of Indian data sovereignty does not end at defensive consolidation. In a strategic pivot, India has begun exporting its digital architecture. The very systems developed to manage domestic scale—the payments rails, identity frameworks, and public digital infrastructure collectively known as the **India Stack**—are now being offered to other nations.

From Southeast Asia to Africa, governments seeking alternatives to Western platform dominance and Chinese state-centric models are studying India's approach. The appeal lies in its hybrid nature: state-backed infrastructure layered with private innovation. Unified payment systems that cost almost nothing per transaction. Digital identity systems designed for scale rather than profit.

This export of digital blueprints represents a new form of soft power. Instead of arms or aid, India offers architecture. Instead of ideology, it offers infrastructure. The Silicon Pulse becomes portable.

For the Global South, the appeal is pragmatic. India's systems were built under conditions of poverty, informality, and diversity—conditions many developing nations recognize. Adopting similar frameworks promises leapfrogging rather than gradual evolution.

Yet this global ambition sharpens the chapter's central dilemma. If India becomes a model for digital governance, the standards it sets will propagate. The safeguards—or lack thereof—will travel too. Exporting the Stack without exporting strong privacy protections risks replicating vulnerabilities at scale.

The chapter closes with an unresolved tension. Data sovereignty is framed as liberation from foreign control. But sovereignty exercised solely by the state can slide into domination. The fortress may keep outsiders out, but citizens live inside it.

As India asserts control over its data destiny, the decisive question remains unanswered: in securing the nation's digital borders, who safeguards the inner freedoms of the individual? The battle for the Indian mind is not only geopolitical. It is constitutional, ethical, and profoundly human.

Chapter 7-The Silent Burnout: Mental Health in the IT Hubs

The Silicon Pulse beats fastest in the glass-and-steel corridors of **Whitefield** and **HITEC City**. These are the nerve centers of India's digital ascent—zones of perpetual light, climate-controlled offices, biometric entry gates, and screens that never go dark. From here, code is written, bugs are fixed, tickets are closed, and global systems remain operational across time zones.

On the surface, these hubs appear engineered for comfort. There are beanbags, free coffee machines, nap pods, and brightly colored motivational slogans lining the walls. Yet beneath this curated aesthetic lies a quieter reality: a workforce stretched across continents, time zones, and expectations, operating in a state of sustained psychological strain. The miracle of India's digital rise, this chapter argues, is underwritten by a largely invisible cost—silent burnout.

7.1 The 70-Hour Debate: Time Poverty in the Age of Permanent Connectivity

The investigation opens with a debate that briefly escaped corporate boardrooms and entered public discourse: the proposition that young professionals should be prepared to work seventy hours a week. Defenders framed it as commitment, discipline, and national ambition. Critics saw it as exploitation disguised as patriotism.

To understand what this debate means in lived terms, one must look beyond weekly tallies and into daily rhythms. For many IT professionals in Bengaluru, the workday begins long before office hours. Commutes of two to three hours through gridlocked traffic are common. The body arrives exhausted before the mind has begun its labor.

Once logged in, the work rarely follows a clean arc. Agile methodologies—Scrums, Sprints, stand-ups—structure the day into continuous accountability. Meetings overlap. Deadlines compress.

Global clients require late-night calls or early-morning check-ins. The workday stretches not because of inefficiency, but because of temporal fragmentation.

This is time poverty. Not the absence of income, but the absence of uninterrupted rest. Sleep becomes negotiable. Weekends become catch-up zones. Vacations are punctured by Slack notifications and "urgent" emails. The boundary between personal and professional life dissolves, replaced by a constant low-level vigilance.

Grind culture normalizes this erosion. Overwork is reframed as ambition. Exhaustion becomes a rite of passage. To disconnect is to fall behind. The fear is not merely reprimand, but irrelevance.

Empirical data supports what anecdote suggests. Rates of sleep deprivation, anxiety, and stress-related disorders among urban Indian professionals have risen sharply over the past decade. Yet these conditions rarely manifest as crisis. They surface as numbness, irritability, chronic fatigue—states easy to ignore, difficult to treat.

The friction here is structural. Digital systems promise efficiency, but global integration demands responsiveness. The miracle of instant service delivery is sustained by human systems that are anything but instant in recovery. The cost is paid not in dramatic breakdowns, but in slow psychological attrition.

7.2 The Replacement Fear: Artificial Intelligence and the Crisis of Professional Identity

Overlaying this exhaustion is a newer anxiety: replacement. For decades, India's IT sector thrived on labor arbitrage—highly educated workers performing complex tasks at scale for global clients. Skill accumulation followed a predictable arc. Entry level coding led to specialization, then management.

Artificial Intelligence disrupts this trajectory. Large language models now write code, debug scripts, generate documentation, and automate testing. Tasks that once defined early career progression are increasingly handled by machines.

The fear is not abstract. Engineers report spending nights learning "prompt engineering," cloud orchestration, or niche AI tools—not out of curiosity, but out of necessity. The pace of change outstrips formal retraining programs. Self-upskilling becomes compulsory, unpaid labor layered atop full-time work.

This produces what can only be described as upskilling anxiety. Careers feel provisional. Expertise feels temporary. The ground beneath professional identity shifts continuously. The worker is not merely competing with peers, but with systems that improve exponentially and never tire.

The psychological impact is severe. Work is no longer a source of mastery, but of perpetual insecurity. Burnout deepens when effort no longer guarantees stability. The question haunting cubicles is no longer "How hard am I working?" but "Will this still matter next year?"

This anxiety intersects dangerously with grind culture. The solution offered is always more effort—more courses, more certifications, more hours. Rest becomes suspect. Pausing feels like surrender.

The friction here is existential. Work is not just income; it is identity. When automation threatens that identity, stress migrates from the workplace into the self. The engineer is forced to continuously rejustify his relevance in a system that no longer promises continuity.

7.3 Bio-Hacking the Grind: Wellness as a Corporate Patch

As burnout becomes undeniable, responses have emerged—not at the level of work design, but at the level of coping. In India's tech hubs, a sprawling wellness industry has taken root. Wearable devices track sleep cycles, heart rate variability, and stress markers. Meditation apps promise focus. Corporate wellness programs offer mindfulness sessions during lunch breaks.

Some professionals go further. Digital detox camps in the Western Ghats offer silence and device abstinence. Bio-hacking communities experiment with nootropics, cold plunges, and quantified self-regimens. The body becomes a system to be optimized.

The irony is difficult to ignore. Technology-induced stress is addressed through more technology. Responsibility shifts subtly from organization to individual. If burnout persists, the implication is personal failure to self-regulate.

Corporations benefit from this framing. Structural overwork is rebranded as a resilience problem. Wellness becomes a perk rather than a corrective. Mindfulness is offered without workload reduction. Yoga sessions coexist with seventy-hour weeks.

This approach produces short-term relief but long-term distortion. Wellness becomes another metric, another obligation. Even rest is instrumentalized. The question is no longer "Am I well?" but "Am I optimized?"

Against this backdrop, a counter-movement has begun to emerge. Quiet quitting, career pivots, and voluntary exits are rising. Some engineers leave for startups with lower pay but greater autonomy. Others exit tech entirely—returning to agriculture, pursuing art, or choosing professions with clearer boundaries.

These departures are not failures; they are signals. They indicate a limit reached—not of skill, but of endurance. The Silicon Pulse, relentless and efficient, has outpaced the rhythms of the human nervous system.

The chapter closes on this recognition. Digital India's success rests on human cognition, creativity, and care. These are finite resources. Burnout is not an individual weakness; it is a system warning. A society that ignores it risks discovering that even the most advanced infrastructure cannot function without minds capable of sustaining it.

Chapter 8-The Shadow Zones: India's Digital Divide

As one moves through the 5G-enabled corridors of **Delhi** and **Mumbai**, it is easy to believe that India has been fully uploaded to the cloud. Contactless payments, app-based governance, real-time navigation, and instant commerce produce an atmosphere of total connectivity. The Digital Miracle appears complete, seamless, and irreversible.

Yet the Silicon Pulse is not a uniform heartbeat. It accelerates in some regions and fades in others. For nearly 400 million Indians, digital India is not a lived reality but a distant spectacle—something overheard on the radio, glimpsed on a neighbor's phone, or promised by politicians. This chapter investigates the Shadow Zones: the geographical, economic, and social spaces where the signal weakens, access collapses, and the future arrives unevenly.

8.1 Tier-3 Realities: Geography as Destiny in a Connected Nation

The investigation begins with a stark contrast. In India's urban centers, mobile penetration exceeds 125 percent, indicating multiple devices per person. In large parts of rural India, penetration struggles to cross 58 percent. This gap is not abstract. It is lived daily, in hills, forests, deserts, and borderlands where connectivity remains intermittent or absent.

In a village in Jharkhand, a high-school student completes his day not by opening a laptop, but by climbing a specific hill at dusk. Only at that elevation does a faint 2G signal appear—just strong enough to download homework assignments sent via a messaging app. Rain disrupts it. Wind interferes. Power cuts end it entirely. Education here is not limited by intellect or motivation, but by topography.

This is the friction of geography. Telecommunications infrastructure follows incentives, not ideals. For Internet Service Providers, building and maintaining towers in sparsely populated or rugged terrain rarely makes financial sense. The return on investment is low, maintenance costs are high, and power supply is unreliable. As a result, vast areas remain digitally marginal.

The consequences extend far beyond education. In a digital-first state, access to welfare schemes, grievance portals, land records, telemedicine, and even courts increasingly presumes connectivity. When the signal dies, citizenship becomes conditional.

Government initiatives have attempted to bridge this gap. Projects like **BharatNet** were designed to connect every village through optical fiber. On paper, progress has been impressive. On the ground, cables are cut, equipment lies idle, and electricity shortages render infrastructure inert. Connectivity requires not just installation, but maintenance—and maintenance requires local capacity that is often absent.

The result is a two-speed India. In one, digital services reduce friction and amplify opportunity. In the other, digitalization introduces new barriers. Geography becomes destiny once again, not because of distance alone, but because the future has been architected around assumptions of access.

8.2 The Gendered Phone: Power, Permission, and Digital Patriarchy

The digital divide is not only spatial; it is social. One of the most persistent and least discussed fault lines is gender. In many rural and semi-urban households, a smartphone exists—but it does not belong equally to all.

Data from the mid-2020s shows that men are significantly more likely to own personal smartphones than women. In villages across **Uttar Pradesh**, women describe a familiar arrangement: one phone per household, controlled by a male relative. Access is conditional, time-limited, and supervised.

This is digital patriarchy. The device that promises empowerment instead reproduces hierarchy. Women are permitted to consume—watch videos, speak to relatives—but are discouraged or prevented from using phones for "serious" tasks such as digital payments, job searches, or information access. The justification is framed as protection: fear of misuse, fraud, or moral transgression.

The effect is cumulative. Without independent access, women are excluded from financial autonomy. They cannot operate bank-linked apps, receive direct payments, or explore online work opportunities. Digital literacy stalls not because of inability, but because of denial.

This exclusion has intergenerational consequences. Mothers without digital access cannot support children navigating online education. Girls grow up associating technology with restriction rather than possibility. In a digital-first economy, this becomes a structural handicap.

The gendered divide reveals an uncomfortable truth: infrastructure alone does not equal inclusion. Social norms mediate access. A tower may stand nearby, but permission remains gatekept within households. The Silicon Pulse does not automatically dismantle patriarchy; it can just as easily encode it.

8.3 Hardware Poverty: The High Entry Fee to the Digital Future

Even where connectivity exists and social permission is granted, another barrier remains: cost. Smartphones, data packs, charging infrastructure—none are free. In a country where a basic smartphone can cost a month's income for a daily wage laborer, digital access carries a high entry fee.

This is hardware poverty. Families must make choices between connectivity and consumption. Data packs compete with groceries. Screen repairs are deferred. Phones are shared across siblings, rationed by time and battery life.

To bridge this gap, a secondary economy has emerged. Refurbished phones circulate through informal markets. Predatory lending apps offer "easy EMIs" for devices, drawing low-income users into cycles of digital debt. The miracle of access arrives tethered to financial vulnerability.

In response, alternative models are emerging. NGOs and local innovators experiment with offline servers, community Wi-Fi, and mesh networks that distribute educational content without continuous internet. These efforts recognize a critical reality: universal connectivity is a goal, not a given.

The chapter concludes with a sobering reflection. Until the Silicon Pulse reaches the last hill in **Arunachal Pradesh**, the forest interiors of **Odisha**, the villages of **Jharkhand**, and the distant edges of **Bastar**, India's digital transformation remains incomplete.

A miracle visible only to some is not transformation; it is stratification. The Shadow Zones remind us that technology does not erase inequality by default. It rearranges it. Whether India's digital future narrows these shadows or deepens them remains an open question.

Chapter 9-The Surveillance Sandbox: Safety vs. Liberty

Inside the control room of an Integrated Command and Control Centre, the abstraction of Digital India becomes tangible. Walls of high-definition screens flicker with live feeds from thousands of cameras spread across streets, intersections, parks, and public buildings. In cities such as **Lucknow** and **Hyderabad**, green rectangles bloom and disappear around faces as pedestrians move through crowds. This is not science fiction. It is real-time Automated Facial Recognition System analysis, operating continuously.

This chapter examines India's Surveillance Sandbox—a rapidly expanding ecosystem of cameras, sensors, databases, and algorithms deployed in the name of safety, efficiency, and modernization. India remains a constitutional democracy, but it is increasingly one in which public life is persistently observed. The friction explored here is not between security and crime, but between visibility and liberty in a society where observation has become ambient.

9.1 The Eye in the Sky: From Smart Cities to Scanned Cities

The surveillance expansion in India is inseparable from the **Smart Cities Mission**. Launched with the promise of technology-driven governance, the program envisioned safer streets, optimized traffic, faster emergency response, and data-informed administration. Surveillance infrastructure became its backbone.

Over the past decade, Indian cities have installed millions of CCTV cameras, many networked directly into centralized command centers. In per-square-mile density, several Indian metros now rank among the most surveilled cities in the world. The logic appears straightforward: more cameras mean more deterrence, faster detection, and better response.

Yet the investigation reveals a shift in purpose. Surveillance is no longer reactive—used to investigate crime after it occurs. It is increasingly preemptive. Live feeds are processed through analytics software designed to flag anomalies: a person standing too long in one location, a vehicle moving against traffic flow, an unexpected crowd forming.

This transition—from observation to interpretation—is crucial. Once AI systems are trained to identify "suspicious behavior," surveillance moves from recording reality to classifying it. The categories embedded in code determine what is noticed and what is ignored.

The friction here is psychological as much as legal. Awareness of constant observation alters behavior. People self-regulate. They avoid gathering, lingering, or expressing dissent in public spaces. This is the chilling effect: freedom constrained not by direct prohibition, but by anticipated scrutiny.

Urban anonymity has long been a cornerstone of democratic life. The ability to blend into a crowd allows experimentation, protest, and unguarded interaction. When anonymity erodes, conformity expands. The Smart City quietly becomes a scanned city—efficient, orderly, and subtly coercive.

The promise of safety is real. Crime detection improves. Emergency response times fall. But the cost is a public sphere where movement itself becomes data, and data invites judgment.

9.2 Predictive Policing: When Tomorrow Is Arrested Today

From surveillance flows predictive policing. Law enforcement agencies increasingly deploy software that analyzes historical crime data to forecast where offenses are likely to occur. Patrols are then concentrated in these "hotspots."

At first glance, the logic is compelling. If crime follows patterns, resources should too. But the investigation uncovers a fundamental flaw: data reflects history, not neutrality.

Crime data is not a mirror of criminality; it is a record of policing. Neighborhoods historically subjected to heavier surveillance generate more data. That data feeds predictive systems, which then justify even heavier policing. The loop closes.

In several Tier 2 cities, predictive systems have resulted in intensified stop-and-search operations in specific localities—often poorer, more crowded, or socially marginalized. Residents report increased questioning, monitoring, and suspicion, not because of individual conduct, but because of algorithmic categorization.

This is bias in code. The algorithm does not create prejudice; it amplifies it. Once embedded, bias gains the appearance of objectivity. Decisions are framed as "data-driven," shielding them from scrutiny.

Predictive policing also alters accountability. When an officer acts on algorithmic recommendation, responsibility becomes diffuse. Was the decision human or systemic? Errors become harder to contest when authority is distributed between code and command.

The deeper danger lies in normalization. When prediction replaces investigation, suspicion precedes evidence. Individuals become potential offenders based on statistical proximity rather than conduct. The presumption of innocence weakens not through law, but through practice.

This chapter's investigation finds no malicious intent in most deployments. What it finds instead is overconfidence—an assumption that more data inevitably produces better justice. In reality, it often produces more efficient inequality.

9.3 The Digital Citizen: Rights in a Permanently Observable Republic

The final section of this chapter moves from command centers to courtrooms and civil society offices. India currently lacks a comprehensive statute governing the use of facial recognition and real-time surveillance by law enforcement. Policies exist. Guidelines circulate. But binding law lags far behind deployment.

This gap creates grey zones. Data collected for one purpose can be repurposed for another. Emergency surveillance can become routine monitoring. Temporary measures can solidify into permanent infrastructure. This phenomenon—function creep—is well documented globally, and India is no exception.

Activists and legal scholars warn that once surveillance capacity exists, restraint depends entirely on institutional culture rather than technical limits. The same systems used to find missing children or manage traffic can be redirected toward crowd control, protest monitoring, or political profiling.

The constitutional question is unavoidable: what rights does the digital citizen retain in public space? Is privacy limited to the home, or does it extend to movement, association, and anonymity?

The state argues necessity. Security threats are real. Urban density complicates policing. Technology offers solutions. These arguments carry weight. Yet rights are not designed for convenience; they exist to constrain power precisely when power is most efficient.

The Surveillance Sandbox represents a trial phase, not just of technology, but of democratic tolerance. Each expansion tests how much observation society will accept in exchange for order.

As green boxes continue to track faces on command-center screens, the central question remains unresolved. In the Digital India of 2025, is privacy a right guaranteed by citizenship—or a luxury relinquished for safety?

The answer will not be decided by algorithms alone. It will be decided by law, vigilance, and the collective willingness to question whether a society that sees everything can still be called free.

Chapter 10-The Tomorrow Protocol: Tuning the Pulse

The investigation ends not at a destination, but at a crossroads. Across the spice markets of Delhi, the biometric queues of Jharkhand, the phishing farms of Jamtara, the gig highways of Bengaluru, and the command centers of India's Smart Cities, one truth has asserted itself repeatedly: the Silicon Pulse is the most consequential force shaping modern India.

It has connected a billion lives with unprecedented speed. It has collapsed distance, time, and transaction cost. It has delivered a genuine civilizational leap. Yet it has also revealed something equally important: technology does not arrive as destiny. It arrives as design. And design always reflects values.

This final chapter moves beyond diagnosis. It does not deny the glitches, shadows, and frictions uncovered in earlier chapters. Instead, it asks the only question that matters now: how should India tune the pulse it has already unleashed?

The answer proposed here is not a retreat from digitization, but its maturation. Not resistance, but recalibration. What follows is **The Tomorrow Protocol**—a framework for a human-centric digital future in which technology remains powerful, but no longer indifferent to the people it governs.

10.1 Beyond the Hype: Reclaiming the Human Element

For more than a decade, India's digital rise has been driven by a borrowed mantra: *move fast and break things*. Speed was valorized. Scale was celebrated. Adoption was treated as virtue in itself. This approach was not irrational; it was necessary in a country burdened by inefficiency, leakage, and exclusion. But speed, once useful, has now become dangerous.

The first requirement of the Tomorrow Protocol is a cultural reset. The next phase of Digital India cannot be measured in downloads, dashboards, or daily active users. It must be measured in **trust**.

A quiet shift is already underway. Within India's developer ecosystem, a new generation of engineers is beginning to reject technological neutrality as a myth. They understand that code is not just functional—it is moral. Every design choice embeds assumptions about users, risk, consent, and value.

This has given rise to what can be described as ethical engineering. Privacy-first architectures, minimal data collection, local processing, explainable algorithms—once dismissed as inefficiencies—are now being re-examined as long-term stabilizers. These developers are not anti-technology; they are anti-carelessness.

The Tomorrow Protocol recognizes this shift and elevates it from niche practice to national necessity. India cannot afford systems that work brilliantly at scale while corroding trust beneath the surface. A society of permanent alerts, opaque denials, and algorithmic anxiety cannot remain cohesive.

Central to reclaiming the human element is **digital literacy as a right, not a privilege**. Literacy can no longer mean the ability to use an app. It must include the ability to question it. Understanding consent, recognizing manipulation, identifying fraud, and knowing when to refuse—these are civic skills in a digital republic.

The protocol therefore argues for digital literacy to be taught alongside reading and arithmetic, from the earliest years, in every school—urban and rural alike. Not as vocational training, but as citizenship education. A population that understands the system is harder to exploit, harder to deceive, and harder to dominate.

The miracle of the next decade will not be faster apps. It will be citizens who know when to say no.

10.2 The Ethical Roadmap: Regulation That Protects Without Paralyzing

The frictions documented throughout this book—surveillance creep, burnout, identity exclusion, algorithmic bias, fraud—share a common trait: none of them can be solved by technology alone. They are governance problems disguised as engineering problems.

The Tomorrow Protocol therefore rejects both extremes that dominate policy debates. On one side lies deregulation disguised as innovation. On the other lies overregulation driven by fear. India needs neither. It needs a **middle path**—firm where rights are concerned, flexible where experimentation is required.

This begins with algorithmic accountability. In a digital society, decisions once made by humans are increasingly made by systems. Loans are denied. Workers are de-platformed. Benefits are withheld. When such decisions are automated, the citizen's right to explanation becomes foundational.

The protocol argues that any system used in high-impact decisions must meet three non-negotiable standards: explainability, contestability, and auditability. A citizen must be able to know *why* a decision was made, *challenge* it meaningfully, and trust that the system itself is subject to independent oversight.

This is not anti-business. It is pro-legitimacy. Systems that cannot explain themselves inevitably lose public confidence.

The Tomorrow Protocol also advances the idea of **Reg-Tech**—using technology not merely to enforce compliance, but to protect rights. Just as surveillance systems can track movement, regulatory systems can track misuse. Just as data analytics can profile citizens, it can also detect corporate abuse, data leaks, and discriminatory patterns.

Regulation, in this vision, is not a brake. It is a stabilizer.

Crucially, the protocol insists that the state itself must be regulated by the same principles it imposes on platforms. Surveillance technologies must operate under clear statutory limits, judicial oversight, and sunset clauses. Emergency powers must expire. Function creep must be explicitly prohibited.

A digital state that demands transparency from citizens while remaining opaque itself will eventually provoke resistance. Legitimacy in the digital age flows in both directions.

10.3 India 2030: A Digital Democracy That Works for Humans

The Tomorrow Protocol does not end with caution. It ends with ambition—grounded, realistic, and earned.

India is uniquely positioned. No other country combines this scale, diversity, institutional complexity, and technological adoption. If Digital India succeeds here—ethically, sustainably, democratically—it offers a blueprint for the world.

The India of 2030 envisioned here is not utopian. It is functional.

An India where identity systems do not merely authenticate, but empower—where citizens carry **portable rights**, not just portable IDs.

An India where connectivity reaches the last village, not as charity, but as infrastructure—erasing the shadow zones that still fracture opportunity.

An India where artificial intelligence augments human labor rather than replacing it—absorbing drudgery, amplifying creativity, and restoring dignity to work.

An India where surveillance exists, but is bounded; where security is strong, but liberty is not conditional.

The Digital India Paradox will not disappear. India itself is a paradox—ancient and modern, chaotic and precise, spiritual and computational. The goal is not to resolve contradiction, but to govern it wisely.

The Silicon Pulse is already beating. The question this book leaves behind is not whether India should be digital. That question has been answered.

The question is whether India will be **human** at digital scale.

If the pulse is tuned with care, restraint, and imagination, it will not drown out the human heartbeat. It will carry it—across markets and villages, servers and streets, into a future that belongs to all.

Chapter 11-The Equilibrium — Humanizing the Digital Frontier

The paradoxes explored in the preceding chapters converge on a single, unavoidable question: can India achieve a *balanced* Digital India? Not a perfect one—perfection is neither possible nor desirable—but a stable one. A system in equilibrium.

Perfection, in this context, is not the elimination of friction, but its intelligent management. It is the presence of harmony between speed and safety, efficiency and dignity, scale and restraint. This chapter serves as a strategic roadmap toward that equilibrium: a future where technology functions as a safety net rather than a snare, and where the Silicon Pulse energizes Indian society without exhausting it.

11.1 The Safety-First Architecture: Rebuilding Trust in a Digital Republic

The first requirement of equilibrium is trust. Without trust, no digital system—no matter how efficient—can sustain democratic legitimacy. India's digital architecture has grown rapidly, but its security philosophy remains largely reactive. Breaches are patched. Scams are countered after damage. Surveillance is expanded first and regulated later.

The Tomorrow Protocol demands a shift from reactive security to **proactive resilience.**

At the core of this shift lies the concept of **Zero-Knowledge Architecture**. In conventional systems, verification depends on exposure: to prove who you are, you surrender your data. Identity databases therefore become treasure vaults—high-value targets whose compromise can cause irreversible harm. Biometrics, once leaked, cannot be changed.

Zero-Knowledge Proofs (ZKP) invert this logic. They allow systems to verify truth without revealing underlying data. You can prove you are eligible, authenticated, or authorized without the verifier ever seeing or storing your raw identity. In a ZKP-based India Stack, the state no longer *possesses* citizen data—it merely validates claims against encrypted proofs.

This is not theoretical. ZKP frameworks are already used in advanced cryptographic systems globally. Their adoption would mark a philosophical shift: from data accumulation to data minimization. If a database is breached, there is nothing meaningful to steal. Trust is no longer enforced by firewalls alone, but by design.

Equally critical is the creation of a **Cyber-Civil Defense Corps**. India has long understood that national defense is not only the responsibility of the military. The National Cadet Corps trains youth for physical resilience and civic responsibility. The digital age demands an equivalent structure.

The book proposes a "Digital NCC": a nationwide program that trains rural and semi-urban youth as *Cyber-Mitras*—trusted local cyber guides. These individuals would not be elite hackers or engineers, but first responders to digital distress. They would help elders verify suspicious calls, guide villagers through safe digital practices, and serve as the human firewall against scams like those emerging from Jamtara.

This approach recognizes a fundamental truth: the weakest link in any digital system is not the code, but the user. Security that ignores human psychology is incomplete. Community-based cyber resilience localizes defense, turning awareness into infrastructure.

Finally, equilibrium requires **Algorithmic Auditing**. Systems used in policing, credit scoring, welfare allocation, and surveillance must not operate as black boxes. The proposal for a **National Board of AI Ethics** is not about halting innovation; it is about certifying legitimacy.

Before deployment, algorithms must be audited for bias, proportionality, and explainability. This does not guarantee perfection, but it establishes accountability. A system that cannot be audited cannot be trusted in a democracy.

Trust, once broken, is expensive to rebuild. A safety-first architecture makes trust durable by design.

11.2 Decompressing the Silicon Heart: A New Deal for India's IT Workforce

The digital frontier is not sustained by servers alone. It is sustained by people. The investigation across India's IT hubs reveals that burnout is not an anomaly—it is structural. The stress experienced by millions of engineers is not a personal failure of resilience, but a design failure of work itself.

The Tomorrow Protocol therefore proposes a **New Deal for Developers**, rooted in structural change rather than wellness rhetoric.

The first reform is a decisive shift from **time-based labor to outcome-based work**. The seventy-hour work week debate is a relic of industrial logic applied to cognitive labor. In software development, productivity does not scale linearly with hours. Fatigue degrades judgment, creativity, and code quality.

Asynchronous work models recognize this reality. If a developer completes a sprint in four focused hours, the system should reward efficiency—not penalize absence. Presence-based monitoring belongs to factories, not knowledge economies. India's IT competitiveness will not be preserved by longer hours, but by sharper minds.

The second pillar is a statutory **Right to Disconnect**. Nations such as **France** and **Portugal** have already recognized that digital trespassing—after-hours emails, messages, and demands—erodes mental health and family life.

India's adaptation must be contextual, but the principle is universal: time off must be legally protected, not socially negotiated. Without such protection, the always-on culture will continue to externalize costs onto families, sleep, and long-term health.

Third, the role of Artificial Intelligence in IT must be redefined. The prevailing narrative frames AI as a cost-cutting instrument—a way to reduce headcount. This is short-sighted. The Tomorrow Protocol insists on **AI augmentation, not AI replacement**.

AI should absorb drudgery: repetitive testing, log monitoring, documentation, routine debugging. These tasks drain cognitive energy without adding meaning. When machines take over the mechanical layers of work, humans can focus on architecture, design, and strategic thinking—activities that are both higher value and less psychologically corrosive.

Burnout is not inevitable in a digital economy. It is the result of misaligned incentives. A decompressed Silicon Heart restores sustainability to the very sector that powers the nation's digital ambitions.

11.3 The Decentralized City: Redistributing the Digital Future

A final source of systemic friction lies outside offices altogether: urban concentration. Bengaluru's traffic congestion and Gurugram's housing costs are not incidental inconveniences; they are structural stressors that amplify burnout and inequality.

The Tomorrow Protocol therefore proposes a **Decentralized City Model** for Digital India.

Technology eliminates distance. Yet India has paradoxically concentrated its digital workforce into a handful of megacities. This concentration inflates rents, lengthens commutes, strains infrastructure, and centralizes opportunity. The result is avoidable human cost.

A human-centric digital frontier must move work closer to people, not force people to migrate endlessly toward work.

The proposal is simple but transformative: incentivize **Tier 2 and Tier 3 satellite IT hubs** in cities such as **Mysore**, **Kochi**, and **Indore**. These cities already possess educational institutions, livable environments, and cultural continuity. What they lack is concentrated digital capital.

Policy incentives—tax benefits, infrastructure grants, remote-first mandates for government IT contracts—can reverse the centrifugal pull of megacities. Distributed work reduces commute-related stress, lowers cost of living, and allows professionals to remain embedded in social support systems.

Decentralization also democratizes growth. Digital wealth no longer pools in a few urban enclaves; it circulates across the subcontinent. The Silicon Pulse becomes distributed rather than congested.

This is not nostalgia. It is resilience. A digitally distributed India is less fragile, less polarized, and more humane.

Conclusion

The Human-Centric Update

The equilibrium envisioned in this chapter does not reject technology. It refines it.

A perfected Digital India is not the fastest one, nor the most surveilled, nor the most automated. It is the one that aligns digital speed with human rhythm.

An India that uses advanced connectivity while respecting the value of disconnection.

An India that digitizes transactions while safeguarding dignity.

An India that governs through data without surrendering conscience.

When the Silicon Pulse synchronizes with the human heartbeat—rather than attempting to outpace it—the paradox resolves itself. Not into perfection, but into balance.

That balance is the true frontier.

And it is within reach.

THE END

Don't miss out!

Visit the website below and you can sign up to receive emails whenever G.K.MENON publishes a new book. There's no charge and no obligation.

https://books2read.com/r/B-A-LZLDF-MRXWI

BOOKS 2 READ

Connecting independent readers to independent writers.

Also by G.K.MENON

INDIA MATTERS
The "Digital India" Paradox
Savarkar The Non-Defeatable
False Prophets of Ambedkarism

The Cognition Series
The Starforge Protocol
The Neural Covenent
Beyond Neural Axis
The Omega Protocol

The Research & Analysis Series
The Manufactured Mind
The Jews The Most Haunted People on Earth

About the Author

G. K. Menon is a writer and independent thinker whose work explores the intersection of technology, power, and human autonomy. Drawing from contemporary debates on artificial intelligence, governance, and ethics, he examines how systems designed to protect society can quietly reshape freedom, identity, and choice.

Rather than focusing on spectacle or rebellion, Menon's writing is known for its reflective, philosophical tone—probing the subtle ways control emerges through convenience, efficiency, and consent. His narratives challenge readers to question modern assumptions about progress, intelligence, and what it means to remain human in an age of optimization.

The Neural Covenant is part of **The Cognition Series**, a collection of speculative works that investigate the future of human thought, responsibility, and survival in technologically mediated societies.

www.ingramcontent.com/pod-product-compliance
Lightning Source LLC
LaVergne TN
LVHW090432210926
848480LV00002B/792
* 9 7 9 8 2 3 3 5 0 5 1 5 7 *